Shine like Stars for Evermore

Color Graphics

Ana Méndez Ferrell

Voice Of The Light

M I N I S T R I E S

LIKE STARS FOR EVERMORE

Publisher: Voice of The Light Ministries / United States of America
Category: Kingdom of God
Design / Edition: Ana Méndez Ferrell
Layout Design: Andrea Jaramillo

Color magazine of the book Like Stars For Evermore,
Color Graphics Collection

www.voiceofthelight.com

1st English Edition 2021, Voice of The Light Ministries - P.O. Box 3418 Ponte Vedra,
Florida, 32004 / U. S. A.

ISBN 978-1-944681-39-5

I thank my Heavenly Father, my beloved Lord Jesus, and His precious Holy Spirit for every revelation laid out in this book. To God alone be all the Glory.

I dedicate this book to all the children of Light that will shine like the stars forever and to this new generation arising, with the sole purpose of being a Light so that God may be known and glorified in the nations.

I also dedicate it to my grandchildren, Leon and Karem, whom I carry in my heart like a flaming torch of God's Love. They will carry the shinning and the banner to many generations.

Shamayim , Raqia

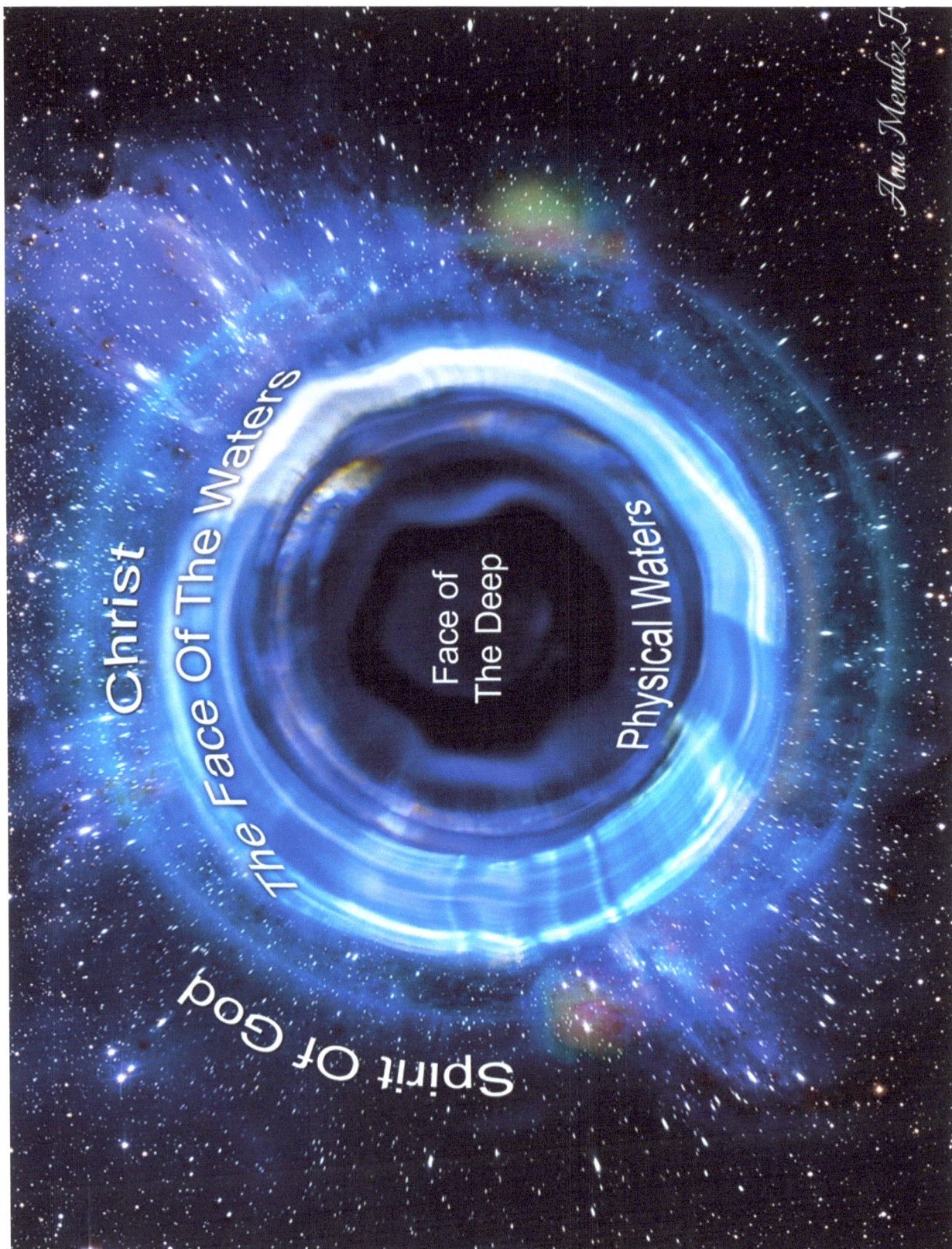

The waters above and the ones below over the face of the deep

As is the heavenly man, so also are those who are of heaven

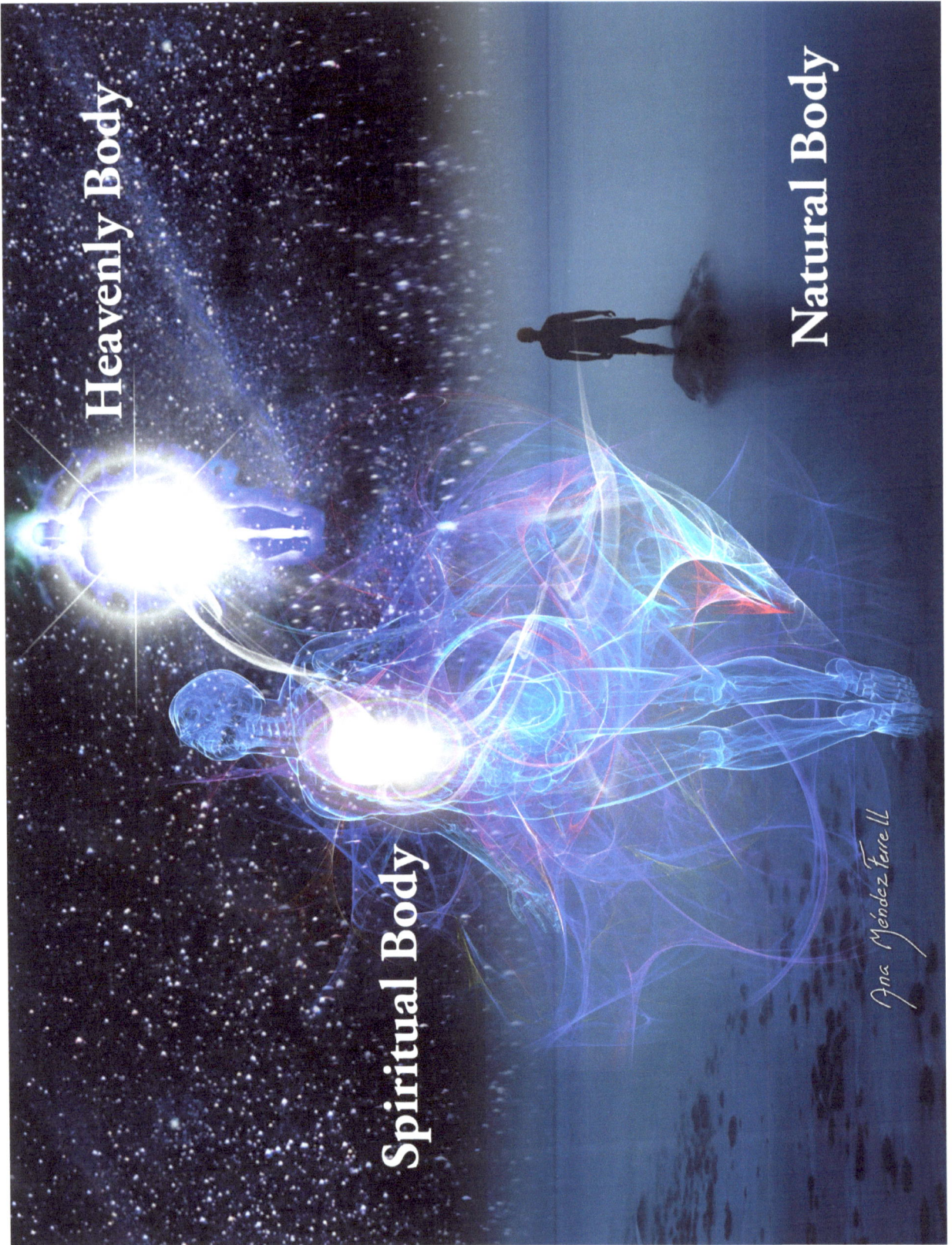

Heavenly Body, Spiritual Body, Natural Body

We are the light and have the power to tear down the false Raqia

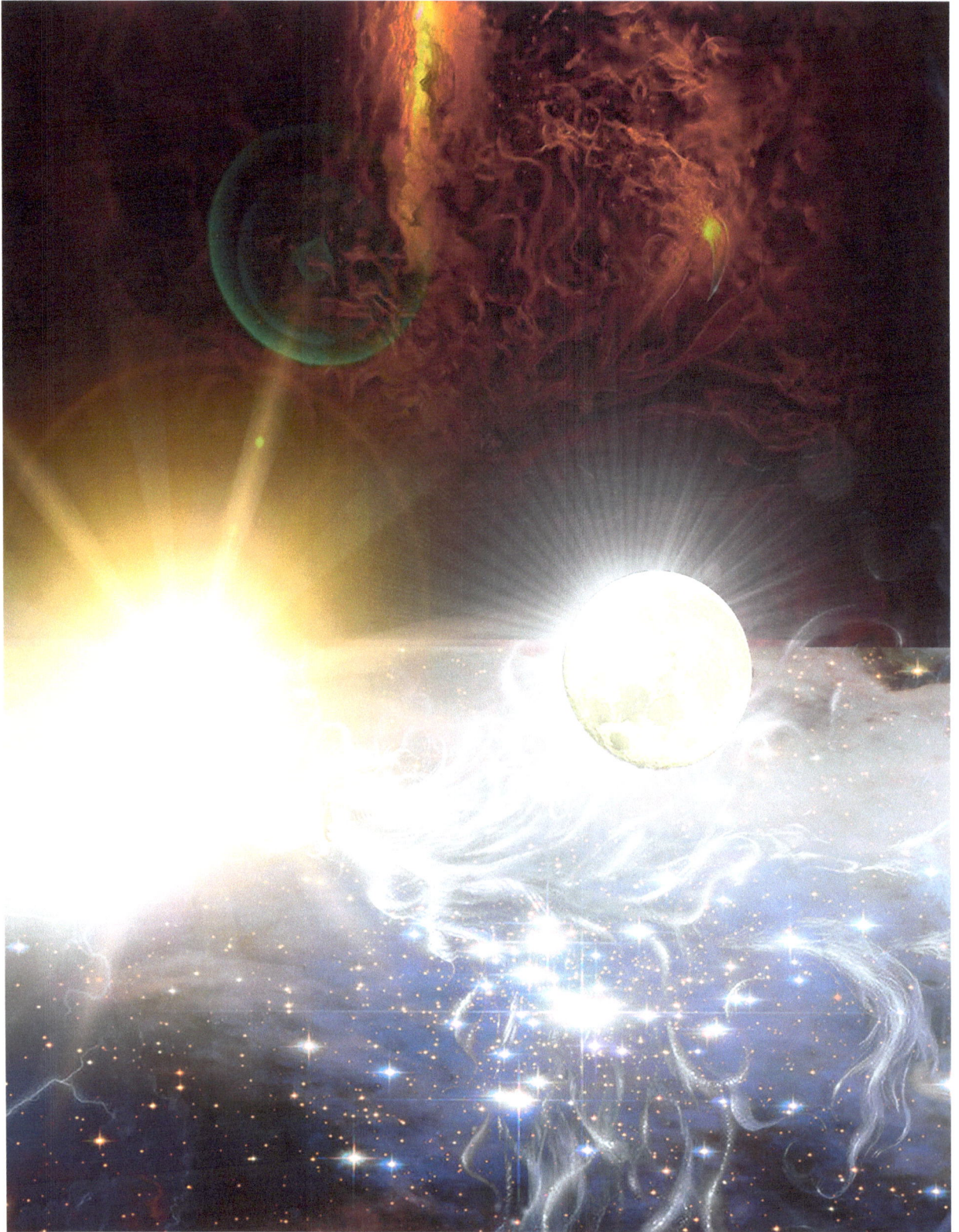

The luminaries rule, separating the day from the night

The four living creatures, the Raqia and God's Throne

The New Jerusalem Covering Our Celestial Being

When I am born again in my heavenly being

My being in Jesus and Jesus in the New Jerusalem

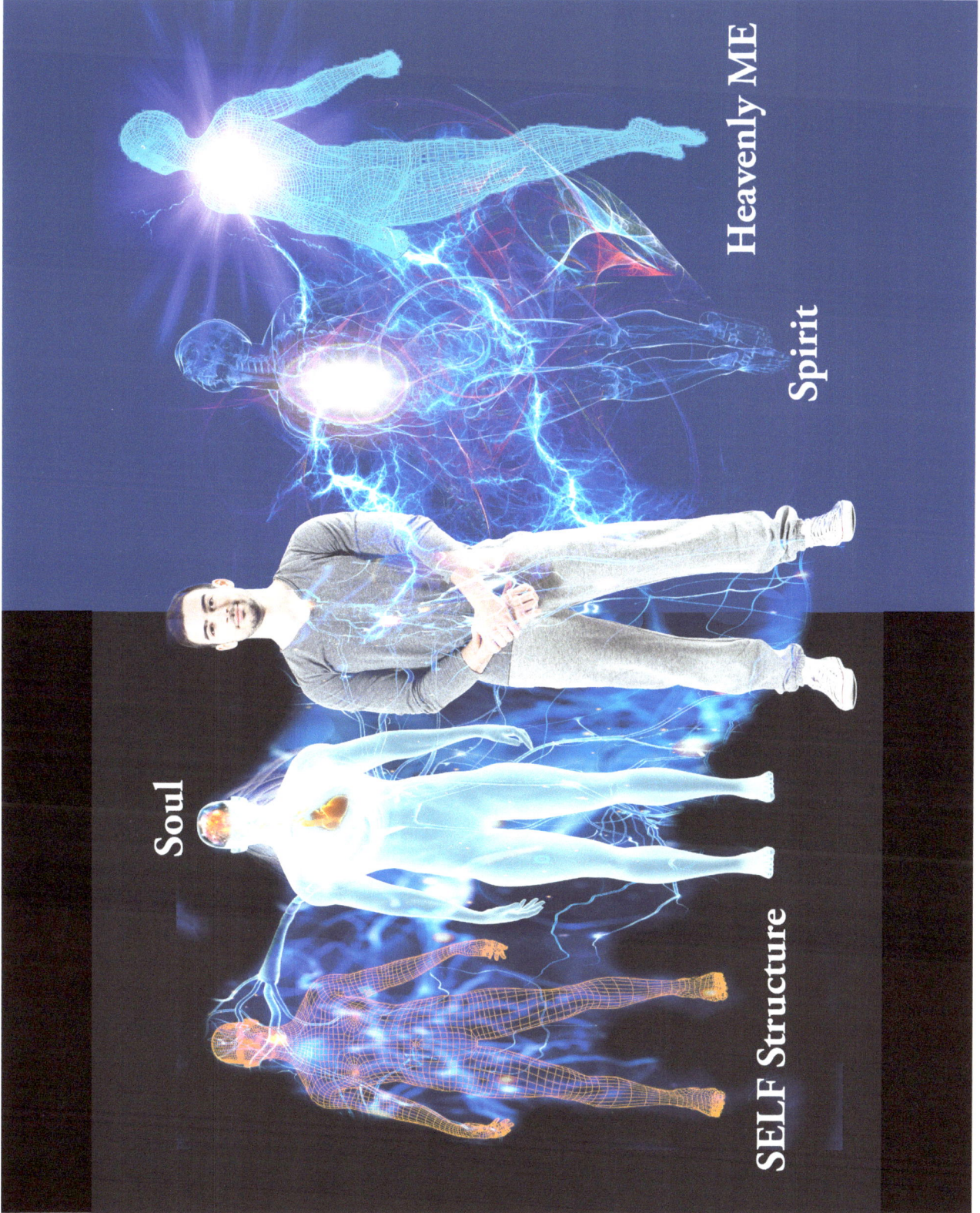

The two personas

We are the doors for the heavenly to manifest on the earth

The Raqia Reflected on The Earth

My heavenly me

Participate in our video course series

Sons Of The Light
Ana Méndez Ferrell
ON DEMAND

The Kingdom Living Through You
A Prophetic Training
Ana Méndez Ferrell
A Bilingual Series
VIDEO ON DEMAND

Prophet Ana Méndez Ferrell
THE SPIRIT OF MAN
The revelation of the most wonderful creation of our inner being

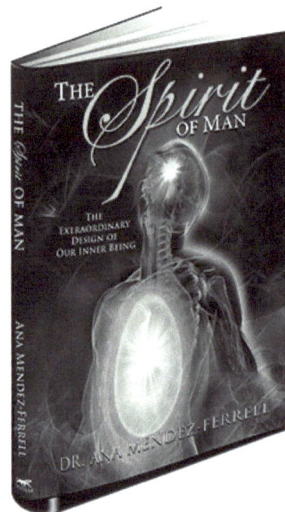

If you enjoyed this book, we also recommend

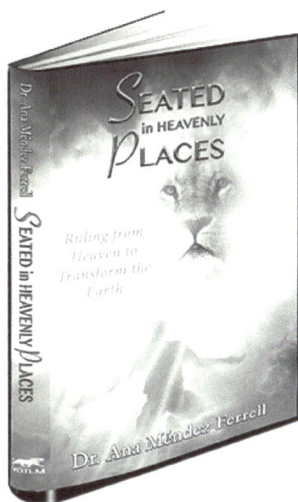

Seated In Heavenly Places

This is a book of Reformation that includes the keys to understanding the Government of God and experiencing His power in our lives. This is a work that challenges you to the very core of your being as the Lord takes you to His throne.

These pages, written by Dr. Ana Méndez Ferrell, will allow you to understand the spiritual realm and help you penetrate the most beautiful places and dimensions of the Spirit.

You will be guided on how to see and know God, not when you die, but HERE and NOW.

Get it today

www.voiceofthelight.com

Watch us on **Frequencies of Glory TV** and **YouTube**
Follow us on **Facebook**, **Instagram** and **Twitter**

www.frequenciesofglorytv.com
www.youtube.com/user/VoiceoftheLight

https://m.facebook.com/AnaMendezFerrellPaginaOficial
www.instagram.com/anamendezferrell
www.twitter.com/MendezFerrell

Contact us today!

Voice of The Light Ministries
P.O. Box 3418
Ponte Vedra, FL. 32004
USA
904-834-2447

www.voiceofthelight.com

like Stars for Evermore

www.ingramcontent.com/pod-product-compliance
Lightning Source LLC
Chambersburg PA
CBHW041428090426
42741CB00002B/90